FARMING TODAY
YESTERDAY'S WAY

FARMING TODAY
YESTERDAY'S WAY

Cheryl Walsh Bellville

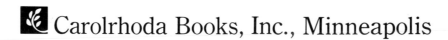 Carolrhoda Books, Inc., Minneapolis

The author would like to thank Pam and Tom Saunders and their children, Molly, Luke, Ivy, and Nell, for their help in the production of this book and for the extra trouble they took so that all phases of the farming cycle could be photographed on their farm.

Thank you also to Kippy Stout, who is pictured in some of these photographs.

Photographs on page 30 courtesy of Rod Bellville.

Words that appear in **boldface** are defined in the glossary on page 40.

LIBRARY OF CONGRESS CATALOGING IN PUBLICATION DATA

Bellville, Cheryl Walsh.
    Farming today yesterday's way.

    Summary: Traces a year of life on a small dairy farm in western Wisconsin where draft horses rather than modern machines do most of the farm work.
    1. Dairy farming — Juvenile literature. 2. Draft horses — Juvenile literature. 3. Dairy farming — Wisconsin — Juvenile literature. 4. Farm life — Wisconsin — Juvenile literature. [1. Dairying. 2. Draft horses. 3. Horses. 4. Farm life — Wisconsin] I. Title.
SF239.5.B45   1984   636.2'142   84-3215
ISBN 0-87614-220-X (lib. bdg.)
1 2 3 4 5 6 7 8 9 10 94 93 92 91 90 89 88 87 86 85 84

For Rod

People have been farming for thousands and thousands of years, and throughout most of that time they have used animals to do the heavy work. At one time oxen supplied most of the pulling power, called **draft power**, on farms. Then in the 19th century, when horses became more available, draft horses became popular because they could work much faster than oxen. In the 20th century, tractors began to replace horses. They were faster yet and could do much more work than horses.

Today most farmers in the United States use tractors, but on a small dairy farm in western Wisconsin there lives a family farming today in yesterday's way.

7

It's July, and Tom Saunders has a lot of work to do in the fields. But before he can get to it, there are chores to be done.

Milk is the main product of a dairy farm, and dairy cows must be milked twice each day all year round. The first milking is done in the early morning, the second at the end of the day.

Tom brings the cows in from the pasture, and each one goes to her regular place to be fed and wait her turn for milking. Because of the large quantities of milk these cows produce, they need extra food besides what they get from grazing. Each of Tom and Pam's 12 milking cows gives about 25-30 pounds (3-4 gallons) of milk each day.

On a mechanized farm, the cows would be fed bales of hay and **silage** from an electrically operated feeder. Tom feeds his cows by hand, throwing down loose hay from the hayloft with a pitchfork and shoveling grain or silage into a wheelbarrow to deliver to the cows. His youngest daughter, Nell, keeps him company.

Modern cows are not built to be milked by hand—their **teats** are too short—so Tom uses a milking machine. After each cow has been milked, Tom pours her milk from the milking machine into a **shotgun can**. The can holds about 40 pounds of milk, or two cows' worth. When it is full, Tom carries it to the milkhouse and pours the milk into a **bulk tank**, where it will stay cool until it is picked up by the milk truck that comes every two days. (On a mechanized farm, the milk would be drawn directly from the cow into a pipeline that would carry it to a bulk tank.) All of the milk from this farm is taken to a cheese factory to be made into cheese.

There are usually four to six calves on the Saunders farm, and some of the milk will be saved for them. The farm's cats will also get a share of the morning's milk.

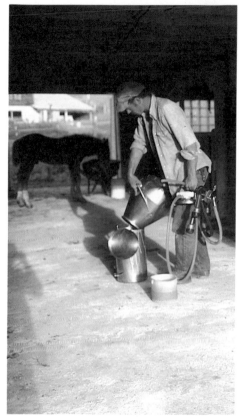

Luke watches while his father cleans the cow's teats before milking her. He and his sister Molly have chores too. They help to feed the livestock and they sweep out the barn.

11

After the morning milking is done, the barn and all of the equipment used for milking must be cleaned, and the livestock must be fed. Hay and grain go to the horses, and pails of feed go to the Saunders' two pigs.

All of these chores—milking, feeding, and cleaning up—will be repeated every evening after supper.

Field work—all the different jobs done to raise crops—is done between morning and evening chores. On most farms today, tractors are used in the fields, but on the Saunders farm, horses supply all the draft power. Horses give the farm a flexible power supply. One horse may be all that's needed for some jobs. Others may require a team of two, three, or four horses.

Horses that are used for work are called draft horses. They differ from riding horses in that they are heavier and stronger. Including **colts** and **fillies**, the Saunders have seven draft horses on the farm right now. They may sell one or two of the young ones, and they often keep other people's horses to train.

14

Ben is harnessed and ready to go.

Before the horses can be hitched to the field machinery, they must be harnessed. The **harness** consists of a bridle, a collar, driving reins, and leather straps that go around the body of each horse. The harness enables the horse to pull the machinery and allows the farmer to control the movement of the horse.

The connection between the horses'
harnesses and the machine to be pulled is
called the **evener** because it evens the load
so that one horse isn't pulling more weight
than another.

16

Earlier this week the farm's fields of alfalfa and grasses were cut. Once cut, the alfalfa and grasses are called hay. In two or three days, when the hay is dry, Tom rakes it into rows called **windrows**.

The machine in the background attached to the wagon is a hay-loader.

The hay-loader, which is pulled behind
the wagon, picks up the hay in the windrows
and dumps it onto the wagon. Tom levels
18

it by hand on the hay wagon and takes it
to the barn where it will be stored until
it is needed to feed the cows and horses.

A pulley-operated hayfork is used to lift the hay from the wagon and up through the haydoor into the barn's hayloft. (On a mechanized farm, the hay would have been baled by a machine in the field, then lifted by an elevator into the hayloft.)

Tom goes through the process of hay-making three times a summer for each of his hay fields. He usually keeps about 15-18 acres in hay.

A week later it's time to cut the oats. The machine Tom is using is called a grain **binder** because it binds (ties) the oats into bundles as it cuts them.

The bundles must then be formed by hand into **shocks.** A shock is made with seven bundles. Six stand on end together, and the seventh is placed on its side across the top. It takes a lot of practice to make a good shock.

In about two weeks the oats are dry. The bundles are then picked up in the fields, loaded onto wagons, and taken to the **threshing machine**.

The threshing machine separates the oats from their stems, which are called straw. It blows the straw into a pile and deposits the oats into a wagon. The straw will be used for bedding for the animals. The oats will be used for animal feed. (On a mechanized farm, the oats would probably be cut with a **combine** which would separate the oats from the straw right in the field.)

Threshing is a big job, and everyone helps out. Traditionally, farm families went from one farm to another to help their neighbors at threshing time. The Saunders still do this, sharing their horses with other farmers. Those farmers, in turn, share their labor and horses with the Saunders.

25

By the time the threshing is finished, summer is coming to a close and everyone is ready for a break. The Saunders family looks forward to the county fair. Sometimes the children march in the parade, and they always enjoy the rides and games, the cotton candy and hot dogs, and watching their father compete in the draft horse competition. The horses are hitched to a

flat device called a **stoneboat** or **skid**. The skid is loaded with concrete weights, and the horses try to pull it a distance of 27½ feet. The team that pulls the heaviest load this distance wins. This competition developed from a time when horses and stoneboats were used to remove rocks from fields.

It is fall now. The leaves are beginning to change color, and by October it is usually time to harvest the corn.

The corn is cut with a corn binder. Then the bundles are loaded by hand onto a wagon and taken to the **silo** where they will be fed into a corn chopper and chopped up—stalks, ears, and all—for **silage**. Silage is naturally preserved chopped corn which is used as livestock feed.

Finally the year's harvest has been completed and winter has come. Work on the farm slows down now, but it never stops completely. Chores must still be done every morning and again every night. All year long, manure is cleaned out of the dairy barns and spread on the fields as fertilizer. Horses work so well for this job—especially in the winter—that some dairy farmers who do their field work with tractors keep a team of horses just for spreading manure. After all, horses are much less likely to get stuck in the snow than are tractors! And they're easier to start on a cold morning.

Although most draft horses don't work as hard during the winter, Ben, Charlie, and Mike still have a big job ahead of them: logging. Many farmers in the north have woodlands on their farms, and there is time during the winter to cut the trees for lumber and firewood. Tom logs his own woods and those of other people in the area.

The trees are cut down and the tops removed from the trunks. The horses skid (slide) the logs (trunks) to a central landing place. There they can either be loaded onto a truck or wagon and taken to a sawmill, or they can be sawed on the spot with a portable sawmill. The tops of the trees are used for firewood.

Horses are good at this work, and they do not damage the ground or the young trees as much as mechanical skidders do.

Ivy gets a ride with her dad on the plow.

Early in the spring, as soon as the ground thaws and can be worked, Tom and his horses begin plowing (turning over the soil) to prepare for the year's crops.

32

After they have finished plowing, Ben, Charlie, and Lady are hitched to a **disc harrow** which will break large clumps of dirt into smaller clumps.

34

When the soil is smooth and fine, Tom hitches Ben and Charlie to a **corn planter** and begins planting this year's corn crop.

When the corn plants are about three inches high, the field is cultivated for the first time. The **cultivator** digs up the soil between the rows of corn. This gets rid of most of the weeds in the field and also loosens the soil around the young plants. The field will be cultivated again before the corn plants are too high to go beneath the cultivator.

One of the most exciting things to happen in the spring is the birth of the year's baby horses, called **foals**. This usually happens in May when the plowing and planting are in full swing. Lady works right up to the time when she has her foal, then rests for three or four days after it is born.

One advantage of farming with horses is that farmers don't usually have to buy new equipment—they raise it. The Saunders have two **mares** (female horses) that are **bred** every year to produce "new" horses.

These foals are raised, **broken** (taught to work), and either used on the Saunders farm or sold to other farmers.

The Saunders also have a **stallion** (male breeding horse) named Ben. Stallions are often difficult to handle, but draft horses are known for their quiet personalities and even stallions can usually be handled without problems. Draft horses are sometimes called "gentle giants" because they are so big and so good natured.

Lady with her one-hour-old foal

It's summer once again. Soon Tom and his team will be putting up hay, and the cycle you have seen in this book will repeat itself.

Why have the Saunders chosen to farm with horses instead of machinery and to do as many things as possible in the old-fashioned way? Some of their reasons have already been mentioned, but there are others, most of which combine economy and a concern for our environment. Horses get their energy from feed that can be grown on the farm, not from expensive oil

products as tractors do. The waste products from horses go back to the soil as fertilizer; the waste from gasoline pollutes the air. The noise made by tractors and other large farm machinery is absent when the work is done by horses, and there is a peaceful-ness in doing field work with a well-broken team. But probably the main reason that people like the Saunders have chosen to farm in yesterday's way is that they just plain like working with and being around draft horses.

Glossary

binder: a machine that ties crops, like oats, in bundles as it cuts them

break: to train a horse. A draft horse that has been broken has been trained to pull heavy loads.

bred: in this case, to have mated a mare with a stallion in order to produce a foal

broken: see break

bulk tank: a large storage tank used to cool raw milk

colt: a male horse younger than four years old

combine: a machine that separates grain from stems as it cuts a crop in the field

corn planter: an implement for planting seed corn in the field

cultivate: to dig up and loosen the soil between the rows of a crop

cultivator: an implement used to cultivate the soil

disc harrow: an implement used to break up large clumps of dirt in a field

draft power: pulling power. A draft horse has been bred and trained to pull heavy loads.

evener: the connection between the horses' harnesses and the implement they are to pull that evens the load between them

filly: a female horse younger than four years old

foal: a young horse that has not been weaned

harness: the equipment that goes on a horse so that it can be attached to an implement or a wagon for pulling

implement: a piece of farm equipment

mare: a female horse over four years old

shocks: bundles of grain that have been stacked together

shotgun can: a large can used to hold milk before it is poured into a bulk tank

silage: naturally preserved chopped corn used for livestock feed

silo: a place where silage is stored

skid: see stoneboat

stallion: a male breeding horse

stoneboat: a sledge or other flat device used for sliding heavy objects over the ground

teats: a cow's nipples out of which milk comes

thresh: to separate the grain from the stems of a crop

threshing machine: a machine that threshes

windrows: rows of mown hay